Contents

The sport 3

Fitness 4

Buying a bike 6
How much to spend? 6
What type to buy? 7
What size to buy? 7

Accessories 10
Helmet 10
Shorts 11
Gloves 12
Boots or shoes 12
Eyewear 12

Maintenance and repair 13
Oiling the chain 14
Puncture repair 15

Basic technical skills 18
Saddle height 18
Steering 19
Braking 19
Gears 19

Intermediate skills 21
Going downhill 21
Climbing 22
The front wheel lift 23
The bunnyhop 24

Advanced skills 25
Drifted corners 25
Jumping 26
Steep downhills 27

Riding 28
Energy food 28
Safety 29
Finding your way 30

Touring 32

Competitive events 34
Downhill racing 34
Cross-country racing 36
Trailquest 38
Dual slalom 39
Trials 40

Training for racing 41
Training calendar 42

Useful addresses 44

Glossary of terms 46

Index 48

Acknowledgements

Text by Brant Richards.

Photography by Steve Behr.

The publishers would also like to thank Specialized for its photographic contribution to this book.

The sport

Mountain biking is one of the fastest growing sports around. At home as much on city streets as they are on a rugged mountain side, mountain bikes are accessible to all; indeed many people are now rediscovering cycling, or taking it up for the first time. Buying a bike, purchasing the accessories and learning how to ride on rough terrain can all be made much easier with some guidance. This book will help you learn the skills you need to conquer challenging obstacles in your mountain biking, be that choosing a bike or setting out on your first cross-country race.

Fitness

Mountain biking is a physically demanding sport, but that doesn't mean that you have to be in tip-top condition before you take it up. Providing you are already physically active, your body will quickly become accustomed to riding your bike, although clearly it isn't wise to start riding if you've suffered chest, heart or other physical problems without consulting your doctor. Certainly if you can jog, walk briskly, swim or do other exercise regularly, then you'll have no problems starting out on a mountain bike.

Set yourself attainable goals when you start to ride. Entering a top-class race only days after you start riding is a recipe for disaster, no matter how fit you are. Mountain biking requires new skills, and uses different muscle groups to other sports, even road cycling. The best training for mountain biking is mountain biking itself. The more you ride the better you will become, in all aspects of the sport, not just in terms of fitness.

Most people will be able to manage a ride of one hour on level ground or gently rolling terrain without too much of a problem. Extended rides over hillier terrain will obviously be harder on the untrained body, but will be attainable with time.

Pre-ride stretching is certainly a good idea to prepare the muscles for exercise. Riding hard without a proper warm-up can lead to pulled tendons or strained muscles. Don't do anything violent, certainly not anything that actually hurts. A calf stretch is a good example: stand with one leg about 30-50cm in front of the other, then hold onto a chair, or lean on a wall. Lean forwards, keeping your heels firmly on the floor, concentrating on the stretch, and breathing out at the same time. Hold this for 15 seconds, repeat it twice, then switch to the other leg. Specialist exercise books and magazines are available which will outline other useful exercises and guide you in your pre-ride warm-ups.

Pressing yourself to do too much too soon could lead to strained muscles and, worst of all, a lack of enthusiasm for your new sport. Take it steady when you first set out!

Buying a bike

How much to spend?

Mountain bikes may seem more expensive than other bikes you have ridden. It's possible to buy a mountain bike for under $100, however it is also possible to pay anything up to $2,500! The reason for their high price is that the bikes have to be strong enough to withstand the stresses that off-road riding can place on a bike, but equally they shouldn't be unreasonably heavy.

Cheaper bikes weigh more because they are made from inexpensive, weak materials which have to be used in greater quantities to build a bike of adequate strength. For example, if the metal used to make the frame tubes is half as strong as that on an expensive bike, you've got to use twice as much of it to make the frame strong enough, which means that the tube weighs twice as much as on the more expensive bike.

The fact is that they have to be expensive to be of a quality that will stand up to being ridden off-road. If you are thinking of buying a mountain bike, and you want to use it off-road, you must spend at least $300 to get a bike that will stay together. Spend $500 or more and you'll get something even more suited to the job.

What type to buy?

There are many different brands and types of bike on the market: frames can be made from steel, aluminium, titanium or carbon fibre; the bike can have shock-absorbing suspension forks, or even be a fully-suspended design with suspension forks and a rear suspension system.

For the first time rider, the best bike is one with either a rigid or a suspension fork. Rear suspension bikes are viable for the beginner, but being more complex they add weight and cost to the bike. If you can afford to spend at least $750, then you will have a good rear suspension bike; cheap rear suspension bikes are just heavy and inefficient.

The mountain bike industry is very 'race led' which means that the bike you buy will probably claim to have some racing heritage. This may put off riders who have no intention of racing, but don't worry. Your mountain bike is capable of doing many different things: touring, racing, commuting and more.

▲ *Front suspension forks*

What size to buy?

Probably the most important thing to ensure when buying a mountain bike is that it's the right size. Buy a bike that's too small and you'll have to find a long seatpost which, if you're heavy, will place a lot of stress on the frame. The key factor when deciding if a frame is the right size is standover height. You should have at least 3in (the width of your palm) between the top of the top tube and the top of your legs, when you're standing with your feet flat on the floor, wearing your riding shoes. Any less than this and not only will you land heavily on the top tube if you jump out of the saddle on a slope, but unless you've got super-long arms you'll be stretched out on the bike. A good starting point for determining frame size is to subtract 12in from your inside leg measurement.

Women have longer legs for their height than men, and so require a slightly shorter saddle-to-handlebar set-up. This can either be attained by choosing a brand of bike with a short top tube, or by changing the stem for a shorter model.

An entry level bike

This is the lowest level of machine that can stand off-road riding without falling apart. Cheaper bikes are available but have weaker frames, unsuitable gearing, or wheels and tires that don't work well off-road.

The bike shown opposite has a comfortable riding position for the first-time rider, which is a little shorter and less of a stretch from handlebar to saddle. Braking is provided with reasonable quality alloy brake levers (rather than the plastic found on cheaper bikes), and gear changing is courtesy of simple-to-use 'twist-grip' style shifters.

An enthusiast's bike

As the price of the bike increases, the quality of the frame and the components increases too. The bike shown opposite has a suspension fork, which allows faster and smoother progress for the rider across rough terrain. The quality of the components on the frame, and the frame itself, also mean that the bike is lighter and yet stronger than cheaper models.

The 'twist-grip' shifters fitted to this bike are a better quality model than those fitted to the cheaper bike, with more durable components and better sealing.

A full suspension bike

This bike can be considered the pinnacle of mountain bike technology. Not only is there front suspension, but the rear wheel is suspended.as well, making progress over rough and rocky ground much faster. The downside is that a full suspension bike will always be heavier than a rigid frame, and also considerably more expensive.

The weight aspect means that they've yet to gain acceptance for the majority of cross-country riders, but for downhill riders who are more interested in a fast and comfortable ride down rough tracks, then full suspension has got the vote.

◀ *Entry level bike*

▲ *Full suspension bike*

◀ *Enthusiast's bike*

Accessories

You'll need more than just a bike and a bit of leg muscle to enjoy the sport of mountain biking. Selecting the right components for you and your bike will mean that you can enjoy the sport much more. Clothing specifically designed for cycling, such as helmets, gloves, shorts and shoes, might not look much different from other items you see in shops, however cycle clothing is cut and designed to be used on a bike, and works far better than cheap imitations.

Helmet

Head injuries are a real possibility if you crash on your mountain bike, and it is vital to wear a helmet. In the US, helmets are rated by two different standards: Snell and ANSI. Each has slightly different criteria for helmet safety, but most people are agreed that Snell is the most stringent. Check inside the helmet for a blue Snell sticker and then check to see if it fits.

Different brands of helmet fit different shaped heads, and it may be that your head shape just doesn't suit a Vetta, say, so try a Bell. Just as you must have insurance for a car, consider this essential insurance for your head.

Shorts

Designed to be worn right next to the skin, with no underwear, it's sensible (and hygienic) to buy two pairs if you're going to ride frequently. Using a synthetic chamois padded insert, cycling shorts don't chafe you when you ride, but allow free movement. Women's shorts are available with seams and shape cut for women's anatomical differences. Lycra blends are the materials of choice, but 'touring shorts' are available which have a baggy appearance, with a suspended inner short. Short liners, a cut-down lightweight version of the bike short, are also on the market, allowing you to ride in conventional athletic wear.

Shorts will seriously improve the comfort on your bike, but don't expect miracles. The human body does require a little 'toughening up' before getting used to life in the saddle, so a little soreness is common. Anything that numbs parts of the body or causes severe chafing should be investigated.

Gloves

When you crash, if you don't land on your head, you'll land on your hands. Without some form of glove on you'll rip your palms to shreds. Mountain bike gloves are available both with and without fingers, and in summer and winter weights. Get a pair to suit the conditions that you're riding in.

Boots or shoes

Though you might think that any general-use athletic shoes would do for cycling, to get the most from your bike proper mountain bike boots or shoes work best. These not only protect your ankles and toes from the abuse of off-road debris, but they also have a sole that lets you pedal hard without the pedals digging into the soles of your feet. They also allow you to use clipless-pedal systems, which are like mini ski-bindings, so your shoes 'click' into the pedals, and 'click' out of them when you twist your heels outwards.

Eyewear

Whether you're riding in wet or dry weather, it's important to protect your eyes from the debris that could fly at you either from the trail or from another rider. Normal sunglasses are a stop-gap measure, but they don't have everything that the mountain biker needs. Lenses should be plastic and not glass so they don't cut your eyes if you crash, and the lens profile should be such that it can stop flying grit from getting in your eyes. Lens material for summer use should be a true UV filter, to limit the chances of contracting a disease of the retina. Simply darkened plastic can be dangerous as it dilates the pupil and allows unfiltered light through to your eye.

Maintenance and repair

Your mountain bike needs care and attention in order to keep it working. Failure to do routine maintenance will result in a bike that wears out quickly, and can become potentially dangerous. Whilst there are operations on your bike that you can only achieve with the correct tools, spotting these problems is simple enough, and either you can buy the correct tools and fix the bike yourself, or get a local shop to do the work for you.

Basic toolkit ▶

Oiling the chain

This is the very least you should do with your bike. After every couple of rides, clean the chain by holding the lowest part of the chain in a rag and rotating the pedals backwards to clean off stuck-on dirt. Then apply the oil to the chain, whilst still spinning the pedals backwards until you've coated the whole chain. Do this when you finish a ride rather than as you're about to leave, to give the oil a chance to soak into the links and pins of the chain, where it's needed to stop metal-on-metal wear.

▼ *Oiling the chain*

Puncture repair

Arguably the most disabling thing that can go wrong with your bike when out on the trail, a puncture renders your bike difficult to ride. It can only be mended with the proper kit, and without that you really are stuck.

Removing the tire

• Remove the wheel from the bike by flipping the quick-release lever on the axle, undoing the cable at the brake, and pulling the wheel out of the frame.

• Work around the tire, pushing the bead of the tire towards the centre of the rim. This loosens the tire from the rim and makes the next stage easier.
• Grip the tire sidewalls between your thumb and fingers, and pull one bead up and over the sidewall of the rim.

• Work around the tire doing this until you can get a finger under the bead, and pull the tire off completely. If this doesn't move the tire, then you'll have to resort to tire levers. Push the tire lever under the tire bead, lever it up onto the sidewall, then push the lever around the circumference of the rim.

Mending the puncture

- Put a little pressure in the tube with the pump, and move the tube section by section past your face, to see if you can feel a jet of air. Don't use water to find the hole unless you absolutely have to, as it makes sticking patches on that much more tricky.

- Check the tube right the way around a couple of times in case there is more than one hole, and check where the hole is to make sure that it isn't a big 'snake-bite' hole, where both sides of the tube are punctured.

- Rub the area around the hole with sandpaper to allow good adhesion. Rub an area bigger than the size of the patch. Blow the rubber dust off the tube, but don't touch the roughened area too much as it weakens the bond.

- Spread the glue thinly on the area, and leave it for a couple of minutes.

- Peel the backing off the patch and apply it to the glue. Rub the patch to improve the bond between it and the tube. Let the glue get to work for a couple of minutes before inflating the tube.

- Put a couple of strokes of air into the tube, as it makes it easier to refit in the tire. Don't inflate the tube outside the tire to check the seal as it might blow the patch off.

- Before you replace the tube in the tire, check that there are no spikey bits sticking through to the inside of the tire. Replace the tire and tube on the rim, reflate and then refit the wheel, and reconnect the brake.

Basic technical skills

Saddle height

Before you set off on your first ride, it's important to set the saddle to the right height. If this isn't correct you can damage your knees, because they won't be extending correctly through the pedalling stroke.

Align the crank-arm with the seat tube, and sit squarely in the saddle, leaning against a wall or partner for support. Place your heel on the pedal and, after loosening the seat-clamp with an allen key, move the saddle up or down until your leg is completely straight at this in-line position. After tightening the allen bolt, check the position with your feet in the correct pedalling position, with the ball of the foot in the centre of the pedal – your leg should be almost straight.

If you find that to get the correct saddle height the post is almost out of the frame (check for the MAX HEIGHT line on the post), or all the way into the frame, then something's wrong. If you need a post longer than 350mm, your frame is too small for you. If you only have 2in of seatpost showing, you have a frame that is too large for you.

◀ *Adjusting saddle height*

Steering

Bicycles are steered by leaning, rather than by turning the handlebars. The faster the bike is going, the less the bars need to be turned. On a road bike you can steer far more by turning the bars, but when you're off-road, turning the bars makes the front wheel 'washout' and understeer in loose corners. Practise this 'leaned steering' on level ground in a wide open space, such as a car park. To make your mountain bike go left, lean to the left, and turn the bars a little to the left as well. To make your bike go to the right, do the opposite. If you're only going slowly, however, significant bar-turning (and balance) will be needed to execute a turn.

Sudden changes of direction are achieved by counter steering: quickly leaning the opposite way from that which you want to go, then steering and leaning the other way. This forces the bike over quicker, tightening the turn.

Braking

Mountain bike brakes are so powerful that it's possible to lock either the front or the rear wheel using just one finger. The front brake is the most important brake on your bike, and the one that you should use most, despite any worries you might have about it pitching you over the handlebars. Pulling hard on the rear brake will simply make the back wheel skid. The rear brake is good for finely controlling your speed, but the majority of the braking force must be applied by the front brake. Don't tug hard on the brake levers, squeeze them. Brakes do not have to be either on or off, they can be used anywhere from fully on, to just rubbing the rim of the wheel.

Find out which is your front and rear brake lever. Typically, the front brake is on the right, but this varies from country to country.

Gears

Your mountain bike has many gears, certainly more than other types of bike. This is because they need to be ridden up steep hills, and must also be able to ride down them. The number of gears (typically 21 or 24) means that there's not a huge jump between each one; you can see how many gears you have from the number of chainrings at the front (usually three), and the number of cogs at the rear (typically seven or eight). Don't be too confused by this; simply consider the bike to have three sets of eight gears. Ride with the bike in the middle chainring at the front, and use the rear gear shifter to change. Only when you encounter something really steep do you need to select the smaller chainring, and equally, when you're riding fast on the flat, the outer chainring is used.

Changing gear should be done when you're not pushing hard on the pedals. Though gear mechanisms will cope with changes under full load, it's better for the chain and gear system if you ease up pedalling pressure when changing.

Intermediate skills

The skills you need to learn when going up- or downhill are based around weight distribution. If your weight is too far forwards, or too far back, the bike will have a tendency to try to roll on the wheel with more weight. Hill climbing with too much rear weight bias will mean that your bike 'wheelies', and too much weight on the front when you're going downhill can mean you falling over the bars (especially when combined with overuse of the front brake).

Going downhill

Dropping your weight backwards stops you flipping off the front when you're riding downhill, but most beginners get into the habit of throwing their weight too far back too soon. When you're hanging off the back of the bike, you can't turn the bars or hold onto the brakes properly, and that makes it more likely that you'll crash. It's far better to stand up off the bike, rather than crouching down low at the back, so you can still manoeuvre the bike properly.

◆ **Key points** ◆

◆ Look down the trail.
◆ Keep weight backwards.
◆ Bend arms.

Climbing

Climbing is all about controlling the weight to get good traction, but not to lighten the front of the bike so much that the wheel lifts off the ground. On gentle climbs traction is no problem, but on steeper slopes there is a battle between traction at the back and wheelies at the front. Crouching down and bringing your upper body closer to the handlebars not only aids power into the pedals, but also stops the front wheel lifting. What isn't a good idea for beginners is to stand up for steep climbs. Use the gears and get the weight over the driving wheel, and you should be able to ride up the steepest slopes.

◆ Key points ◆

◆ Pedal smoothly.
◆ Keep weight forwards.

The front wheel lift

Probably the most useful of any off-road skill is the ability to lift the front wheel of the bike over obstacles, allowing a far smoother passage along any track. To lift the front wheel off the ground, you need to transfer your weight quickly to the back wheel, by pushing down hard on the pedals and throwing your weight backwards. This will either unweight the front wheel, or, if done hard enough, lift it off the ground completely.

Keeping your weight like this whilst still pedalling allows you to 'wheelie', not an essential off-road skill, but one of the first bicycle 'tricks' most people learn!

◆ Key points ◆
◆ Keep weight backwards. ◆ Cover the rear brake. ◆ Keep pedalling.

The bunnyhop

There are times when you need to lift the bike completely off the trail, to clear a pothole, log or similar obstacle. Though this might seem like defying gravity, the bunnyhop is a simple skill to learn and will come in useful.

There are several techniques to bunnyhopping, but the simplest to grasp is a backwards weight shift (as in the front wheel lift), followed by the rider simply jumping in the air and pulling upwards on the pedals to lift the bike clear of the ground. Clipless pedals assist this technique, as the rider can jump upwards and the bike lifts off the ground easily.

Other techniques of bunnyhopping use a wheelie then a fast front weight shift to lift the bike clear of the ground, but these are advanced techniques used by skilled riders to attain heights of 40in or more.

◆ Key points ◆
◆ Bend arms. ◆ Pull upwards. ◆ Bend knees. ◆ Check landing.

Advanced skills

Professional riders use skills that are more advanced to allow them to travel faster over rough terrain. Travelling at higher speeds, the bike responds differently to the rider input. These techniques should only be practised when you've mastered the basic and intermediate skills.

Drifted corners

Locking the back wheel when riding slowly will simply make the bike stop, but shifting your weight forwards and locking the back wheel can be a way to 'rear-wheel-steer' the bike. It's a technique that's used by downhill racers to make the bike turn without having to steer it through a corner. The rear wheel pushes the bike around, so avoiding having to turn the handlebars excessively and risking the possibility of the front wheel breaking traction and sliding.

At high speeds and on the right surface it's even possible to achieve a rear wheel slide without using the rear brake to initiate the slide. World-class riders can slide a bike through a corner with both wheels slipping; something that would result in the average rider ending up in a heap on the floor.

◆ **Key points** ◆

◆ Keep foot out.
◆ Keep weight on outside pedal.

Jumping

Hitting bumps in the trail at speed will make your bike leave the ground. Hitting bigger ramps will make you positively fly skywards. However some riders spend all their time performing jumps, going for spills and thrills rather than setting out for a ride.

Jumping at its simplest is just hitting a ramp fast, and letting the momentum of the bike do the rest. To jump higher still, adding a bunnyhop at the point of take-off projects the bike further into the air. The key to jumping well is to be relaxed on the bike, and to cushion the landing by absorbing the impact on the ground by bending your arms and legs. Suspension systems are fine, but they can't match the human body.

Once you have the skills to jump consistently, it's possible to add extra style, for example by twisting the bars in the air (and straightening them for landings!). Other tricks include one-footed, no-footed, one- and non-handed jumps . . . extreme riders keep inventing more variations on the standard 'jump' to make increasingly dramatic moves.

◆ Key points ◆

- ◆ Pull up (as bunnyhop).
- ◆ Keep knees and elbows bent.
- ◆ Check for landing.

Steep downhills

Keeping your weight backwards and descending a slope slowly is fine if you're out in the hills, but downhill racers use more aggressive techniques to travel downhill faster. Standing up off the bike, and barely braking at all, they lift the bike over obstacles by using weight shift skills like those in the bunnyhop and the front wheel lift. Keeping a higher speed when travelling downhill makes the bike roll through obstacles smoothly, skipping through things that may have caused it to crash at a lower speed. Obviously this 'speedier' approach isn't something you should try until you have all the required handling and braking skills required.

◆ Key points ◆
◆ Cover brakes. ◆ Bend elbows. ◆ Bend knees. ◆ Keep weight backwards.

Riding

Energy food

For short mountain bike rides, it's not necessary to worry about eating on the trail, but for rides of more than an hour and a half, it's worthwhile taking along some type of food to stop you flagging in the final miles.

Whilst a regular marmalade sandwich or piece of flapjack will work admirably, there are special foods available to help you perform better on a ride. Specific 'energy bars' get themselves into your bloodstream quickly, to give you the energy to carry on riding. The marmalade sandwich will do the same job but won't be absorbed by your body as quickly, and even when it is, the sugar and fat contained in the sandwich won't fuel you properly. Energy bars get around this by having the right amounts of fats, the right types of sugars and other nutrients to power you onwards. It might sound like hype, but it really works!

Safety

Mountain biking is a dangerous sport, and can lead to injury. Potentially there's the possibility that you could crash and lie injured in an inaccessible location. For that reason it's not advisable to ride alone in remote areas, but when this can't be avoided, ensure that you leave details of your route and an expected time of return with someone. For big wilderness rides this should be a detailed assessment, but if you're just off out for a ride on your own, telling your neighbour you should be 'back in about an hour' could save your life if anything untoward happens.

Not taking adequate spares or tools can also be potentially dangerous. Puncturing in cold, wet weather, miles from shelter is an invitation for hypothermia to set in. Ensure that you take spare tubes, a pump, allen keys and a chain tool. This should ensure that you can fix most trail problems.

Keeping your bike in good shape means that you're less likely to suffer a failure, and riding with a degree of caution on technical terrain will mean that you don't crash and sustain damage to you or your bike. Equally, not eating properly and suffering from exhaustion is a potential disaster.

Emergency energy food, sufficient tools and planning mean that there's every chance of you getting back from even the hardest challenge in one piece!

Finding your way

Maps are quite simple to work with, providing you take some time to set them up properly. Line up the map with the ground. Use known landmarks to point you in the right direction, and move the map so that it's in the same orientation as you want to go.

Contour lines are the indicators of altitude on a map. They're shown as brown lines that follow points of equal height around a hill. It's like the land has been sliced to equal depths. Every line is an increase of 10m, and the cleverer amongst you will have deduced that the closer the contour lines are together, the steeper the hill. Keep away from areas where the map is very brown!

Compasses aren't needed for most trail-riding, but in extreme conditions they do help you 'set' the map more accurately. If you're lost in the wilderness, it's comforting to know that you've got the map aligned correctly, and you're not riding the wrong way up the wrong track.

Touring

Your mountain bike can be your passport to the world. Traditionally, cycle tourists have used dropped handlebar bikes, but the mountain bike with its strong wheels, powerful brakes, excellent gear range and comfortable riding position, is becoming the bike of choice for people setting off to ride to the furthest reaches of the world.

A basic luggage-carrying system of a rack, panniers and a handlebar bag will carry all you will need for most trips. What you take with you depends on where you're going, what you're doing for accommodation and so on. It is wise on extended tours to take two pairs of cycling shorts, to allow you to wash one pair and wear the other. The thought of riding for a couple of weeks in hot climates with the same pair of shorts on doesn't bear thinking about.

The standard mountain bike should be adapted slightly for touring long distances. A set of bar ends are a useful addition, giving several alternative riding positions to avoid being cramped in a single position. Narrow profile, lighter-tread tires make better progress on roads; it's even possible to obtain slick tires for mountain bikes, making them as efficient (in rolling terms) as a road bike.

If you have to get to your destination by plane, it's still possible to take your bike. Packed either in a strong box, or in a specialist bike-bag, journeys on train or plane are trouble-free. Remove both wheels, the handlebars and the rear derailleur, pad the frame with pipe lagging or bubble-wrap, and the bike will arrive at its destination intact. Rebuilding will be a ten-minute affair. Most airlines won't charge for bike transportation as long as you keep within their considerably generous luggage allowance; however domestic flights in the US (when not part of an international flight) charge $50 per bike.

Competitive events

Downhill racing

Downhilling is one of the strongest areas of competitive mountain biking: it's so much fun, and it's a real test of skill rather than of total aerobic fitness. It's a very different sort of fitness to that required in cross-country racing, and as a result downhilling has its own set of riders who will compete only in this field.

The race itself is a time trial. Riders are usually seeded in qualifying runs before the main race. More often than not it's a one-run do-or-die race. Any mistakes, mechanical failures or punctures don't matter. You get one run down the hill to post your time, and that's that. It might seem a tough way to decide a race, but at the end of the day the best man wins, because his bike stays together, he doesn't crash and he rides as fast as possible.

It's a very technical sport, both in terms of the skills required to succeed and the level of equipment needed. As the courses have developed in severity, notably in Europe, the type of equipment used has changed.

Nowadays, world-class downhilling practically demands full suspension, with six to eight inches of wheel travel, disc brakes and puncture resistant tires, and the resulting bike looking like a motorbike without an engine. They are dedicated downhill machines, and are quite unsuitable for riding in a cross-country race. Though cross-country full suspension bikes exist, the downhill bikes have longer travel, with stronger components used in their construction. Suspension forks have extended stanchions, and clamp at the top and bottom of the steerer tube for extra stiffness. Indeed some of these forks are so strong, they can easily rip the front off a conventional bike in a crash. Downhill frames are built far stronger, to withstand the extra loads imposed on them.

Disc brakes are increasingly used, as they give fade-free performance and don't rely on the wheel rim for braking. A crash or bad landing can put rims 'out of true', which would mean that they'd rub on conventional 'cantilever' brakes.

Bars and stem are also unconventional. The saddle is used as a support, not to sit on, and will be low to keep it out of the way of the rider, giving them room to move on jumps and over obstacles. Handlebars are higher and wider than on cross-country bikes, giving better control and a position that allows the front of the bike to be lifted more easily.

The tires will generally be large and heavy-duty to give superb grip. Pressures are high to avoid pinch-punctures, though some racers use puncture-resistant tires with airless inner tubes.

▼ *Adapting a standard bike for downhill*

Cross-country racing

Typically, a cross-country mountain bike race will take place on a four- to six-mile circuit. Certain areas dictate different lengths of circuit, but generally this is the norm. The racers don't all compete in the same race, but are split into age and ability classes.

Cross-country races have a mass start, with the field separated into their relevant categories. The fastest riders will set off first: in a Pro level race the Pro riders will go first, and race organisers may well run the Expert riders two minutes behind them. Typically, a Sports race will have the whole circuit to itself, as that class has the largest number of entrants.

During the race no technical assistance is allowed. Any mechanical problems the riders may have must be fixed by themselves, including punctures and broken equipment. The only outside help allowed is that competitors may be supplied with food and drink; important in a race that may last up to four hours.

A cross-country race bike looks like its rider – thin, lean and tuned for maximum performance. Every last bit of weight will have been trimmed from the bike, with the very best equipment used to enable the bike to perform to the full, and not hamper the athlete.

Though large tires give a better grip, racers usually run on some of the narrowest section tyres around, due to their lighter weight and decreased rolling resistance on hard tracks.

Racers often use a low handlebar position, putting themselves in an aerodynamic tuck, and making sure that they have a good position for powering up the steep climbs. The fact that this sort of position may cost them a little time on the technical downhills isn't too important. Races are usually won on the climbs, where a minute or so can be gained; a few seconds is all that's at stake on the downhills.

Don't imagine that cross-country racers are no good at downhilling; riding these narrow-tyred bikes downhill fast takes a great deal of skill.

The frame of the bike will usually be made from lightweight steel, aluminium or titanium tubing. Rear suspension is sometimes used on cross-country race bikes, but more often the frame will be of a standard configuration. Most racers use a lightweight suspension fork due to the increased comfort that they offer, and also the increase in downhilling speed.

◀ *Cross-country race bike*

Trailquest

The competition closest to the sort of riding most people do is the 'trailquest'. Gaining in popularity in many areas, it offers a very different sort of mountain bike competition that suits older riders with real mountain and outdoors experience. That said, there are many younger people taking part in these events and they are going to grow in popularity.

Exact details vary, but most events run something like this: competitors are given map references of checkpoints in a given area, say 30 miles by 30 miles. These checkpoints are also allocated points, depending on their remoteness. Teams must ride around, visiting checkpoints, collecting points, and then (and this is the tricky bit) get back to the start within a given time or face having points docked for being late. Some events, like the Polaris Challenge in the UK, even include a remote overnight stop, which means that competitors not only have to get around the course, but they have to do it carrying all their equipment and food as well.

▲ *Trailquest competitor at a checkpoint*

Dual slalom

Like an extreme downhill event, dual slalom pits two riders on twin-track marked courses in an elimination style race to decide who goes through to the next round. Courses can vary in duration from 20 seconds to two minutes or more, depending on the area of hillside available, the spacing between the gates and the whims of the organiser.

Slalom courses are like BMX tracks unravelled and laid out down a hill. Berms (banked corners), jumps and ditches are all popular features that course designers will dig into the course.

Riders that excell at dual slalom typically come from a BMX or mountain bike downhill racing background. However, the bikes for dual slalom are quite different to those for downhill racing. Generally they're small, short, and with no rear suspension, to give the riders the speed and power to sprint hard out of corners. They're also light, so that they can be jumped easily, and will have extremely powerful brakes so that riders can leave slowing down as late as possible. Front suspension forks will be used, with high, wide downhill-style handlebars.

Trials

This type of mountain bike competition is the furthest away from what most people would call 'proper' mountain biking. Here, riders try to ride through marked sections without putting a foot down. The sections aren't just simple bits of trail, but can be strewn with logs, rocks, steps, adverse cambers, bankings, anything at all that can make riding difficult. The sections aren't timed, but points are accrued for faults being made, the winner being the rider with the least number of points.

As a result of the difficulties of the sections, many riders don't actually 'ride' their bikes in the normal way. Instead, they lock both wheels using the brakes, and hop their bikes around to make progress. Hopping allows forwards, sideways and even backwards motion (though travelling backwards can itself be a fault in some competitions).

Trials are the cheapest area of competitive mountain biking, and can be done on any standard bike, with the most skilled rider usually winning. The bikes are important at the highest levels of the sport, but many riders simply use stock bikes with good tires, powerful brakes, flat pedals and the middle and outer chainrings removed to give better ground clearance on obstacles.

Training for racing

Racing mountain bikes does require a degree of training. That's not to say that everyone who enters a mountain bike race must be in peak physical condition, but in order to do well you need to be in as good shape, if not better, than other people in your race class.

The level of training required, and the regimentation of that training, depends largely on the level you want to attain, how naturally fit you are, and how dedicated you are to keeping to your training programme.

There are many different approaches to training, some based on real on-the-bike work, others based around more closely monitored turbo-training, where pulse monitors and cadence meters are used to give your body a very specific work-out.

To succeed at the highest levels of the sport, this type of fine-tuning is required; the kind of training that can only be successful if monitored carefully, with the help of a professional coach. Your coach will provide you with experience, monitor your performance by means of resting pulse rates and be better able to analyse your mental state.

Left to your own devices, overtraining is a problem that can occur, leaving you vulnerable to infection from colds and similar ailments. You can't train properly due to being too tired, and your training simply makes you go slower every session. Rest is as important in a training regime as exercise. Ride hard every day and you'll get fitter, but keep riding hard and you'll become tired and your performance will decrease. Training properly means timing these rest and exercise sessions to get the most from your body.

Training calendar

Training for a season of mountain bike racing requires a three-stage plan.

Throughout the winter (October through January) you should concentrate on putting in long rides of a medium level. Ensure you're well rested during this time, and even spend time in the gym working on muscle groups that are under-developed.

From January to the start of the racing season (around the end of March in most countries), more specific training can be carried out. The long rides shouldn't be abandoned, but shorter, harder rides should be included in the training programme; rides that emulate the kind of efforts that are likely to be involved in cross-country racing. As the start of the season approaches, you should have built up the more intense part of the training, before resting for several days before your first competition.

During the race season it's possible to ride every weekend at race pace. And, without a doubt, the best training for racing is racing itself. Again, the importance of rest can't be overstressed. Without it, you'll run out of energy mid-season, and possibly fall foul of injuries.

Useful addresses

Associations

International Mountain Biking Association (IMBA)
P.O. Box 7578
Boulder, CO 80306
303 545 9011
email: imba@aol.com
website: www.imba.com

The mission of the IMBA is to promote mountain bicycling opportunities through education in environmentally sound and socially responsible riding practices and land management policies. IMBA participates in the national efforts to establish and maintain trail networks. It co-ordinates information for 300 affiliated regional clubs across the United States. IMBA publishes a newsletter, the IMBA Trail News, six times yearly.

National Off-Road Bicycle Association (NORBA)
1 Olympic Plaza
Colorado Springs, CO 80909
719 578 4717

NORBA's chief responsibility is to regulate competitive off-road mountain biking in the United States.

Outdoor Recreation Coalition of America (ORCA)
P.O. Box 1319
Boulder, CO 80306
303 444 3353
email: info@orca.org

The mission of ORCA is to preserve and promote the human-powered outdoor recreation industry.

Mountain Biking Publications

Bike
33046 Calle Aviador
San Juan Capistrano, CA 92675

Mountain Bike
Box 7347
Red Oak, IA 51591-0347
800 666 1817

Dirt Rag
181 Saxonburg Road
Pittsburgh, PA 15238
412 767 9910
email: dirtrag@aol.com

Glossary of terms

Aheadset The trade name of the most popular headset design, which uses an unthreaded steerer tube, with the stem clamping onto it (rather than inside it).

Bottom bracket The bearing that the cranks spin on, held in the bottom bracket shell.

Butting A metal component that has the wall thickness or section increased in a step is said to be butted.

Chromoloy The high strength steel alloy used in bicycle frame construction.

Derailleur The mechanism that pushes the chain across the sprockets or chainwheels when a shift lever is moved. Also know as a 'mech'.

Dropout The plate welded to the frame or forks, where the wheels locate into the frame.

Elastomers Synthetic rubbers that have elastic properties. Used in suspension forks as a spring and damping medium.

Headset The bearing in which the fork steerer tube rotates, contained in the headtube.

Indexing Gears which click from position to position, allowing easy selection of the right one.

Seatpost The tube that is clamped in the frame and supports the saddle.

Shifters The levers on the handlebars which allow you to change gear.

Shimano The Japanese component manufacturer which has almost total market dominance on production bikes. Makes good reliable equipment.

SPD The original mountain bike clipless pedal system, made by Shimano.

Sprockets The cogs at the rear of the bike driven by the chain.

Stem The welded tube assembly connecting the handlebar to the front fork.

Titanium The oft-hailed wonder metal of the modern age. Very expensive, light and strong.

Index

accessories 10-12
advanced skills 25-7

braking 19
bunnyhop 24
buying a bike 6-9

chain 14
climbing 22
compass 30
competitive events 34-40
cost 6-9
cross-country racing 36-7

downhill 21
   racing 34-5
   steep 27
drifted corners 25
dual slalom 39

'energy bars' 28
enthusiasts bike 8-9
entry-level bike 8-9
eyewear 11-12

fitness 4
food 28
frame 6-9, 37
front wheel lift 23
full suspension bike 7-9, 34

gears 19
glossary 46
gloves 10-12

helmet 10-11

intermediate skills 21-4

jumping 26

luggage 32

maintenance 13-17

overtraining 41

puncture repair 15-17

rear suspension bike 7, 37
repair 13-17

saddle height 18
safety 10, 29
seatpost 7, 18
shoes 10-12
shorts 10-11
size of bike 7
steering 19
stretching 4-5

technical skills 18-19
tools 13, 29
touring 7, 32
trailquest 38
training 41-2
   calendar 42
trials 40
'twist-grip' shifters 8

useful addresses 44-5

weight distribution 21-7